AWAY WITH WORDS

Young Writers' 16th Annual Poetry Competition

It is feeling and force of imagination that make us eloquent.

How can I not dream while writing?
The blank page gives a right to dream.

YoungWriters

Shro

Edited by M:

 Young**Writers**

First published in Great Britain in 2007 by:
Young Writers
Remus House
Coltsfoot Drive
Peterborough
PE2 9JX
Telephone: 01733 890066
Website: www.youngwriters.co.uk

SB ISBN 978-1 84602 832 8

Foreword

This year, the Young Writers' *Away With Words* competition proudly presents a showcase of the best poetic talent selected from thousands of up-and-coming writers nationwide.

Young Writers was established in 1991 to promote the reading and writing of poetry within schools and to the young of today. Our books nurture and inspire confidence in the ability of young writers and provide a snapshot of poems written in schools and at home by budding poets of the future.

The thought, effort, imagination and hard work put into each poem impressed us all and the task of selecting poems was a difficult but nevertheless enjoyable experience.

We hope you are as pleased as we are with the final selection and that you and your family continue to be entertained with *Away With Words Shropshire* for many years to come.

Contents

Jack Peters (14)   35
Kirsty Arscott (13)   36
Kate Watton (13)   37
Oliver Vincent (13)   38
Andy Lee (12)   39
Camila Burns-Roa (13)   40
Adam Chell (13)   41
Simon Chell (13)   42
Alex Nicholas (13)   43
Laurence Riley (13)   44
Matthew Pollard (13)   45
Suzanne Turner (13)   46
Americk Pamma (13)   47
Benedict Leader (11)   48
Frances Lacey (11)   49
Verity Louise Harris (11)   50
Emma Simpson (12)   51

Newport Girls' High School
Emily Hughes (11)   52
Alice Roman (14)   53
Hannah Partridge (13)   54
Samantha Brizuela (14)   55
Camilla Crawshaw (16)   56
Harriet Boxley (11)   58
Hannah Mitchell (11)   59
Alice Moreton (11)   60
Jenny Rowe (11)   61
Eleanor Lane (12)   62
Heather Clarke (17)   63

Rhyn Park School & Performing Arts College
Jessica Bellingham (11)   64
Jess Austin   65
Elle Hughes (11)   66
Bradley Coombes (11)   67
Ashleigh Birks (11)   68
Gareth Jones (11)   69
Carlee Louise Hands (11)   70
Daniel Whittall   71
Luke Wotton (11)   72

Zac Martin 73
Jessica Birch (11) 74
Grant John Drury (11) 75
James Griffiths (11) 76
Ryan Gibson (12) 77
Michael Evans (12) 78
Kieran Evans (12) 79
Sally Beddow (11) 80
Caitlin Roberts (11) 81
Hannah Jones (11) 82
Lucy Minter (11) 83
Jade Wickenden (11) 84
Chloe Roberts (12) 85
Sophie Knight (11) 86
Rosie Evans (11) 87
Selina Ellis (11) 88
Rebecca Adams (11) 89
Matthew Henderson (11) 90
Adam Thomas (12) 91

The Mary Webb School

Eleanor Hughes (14) 92
Jack Titley (14) 93
Richard Nicholson (14) 94
Amy Betton (15) 95
Amy Finnigan (14) 96
Jan Ashley (15) 97
Bess Robson (14) 98
Molly Sullivan (14) 99
Karla Giles (14) 100
Abbie Sylvester (14) 101
Alex Williams (14) 102
Sarah Pinches (14) 103
Brittany Fisher (14) 104
Tim Robinson (15) 105
Abigail Best (14) 106
Alice Campion (14) 107
Polly Osborne (14) 108
Mollie Newbury (14) 109
Sadie-Beth Holder (14) 110

The Priory School

The Poems

The Dinosaur Age

T eeth like jagged knives
H uge, tall dinosaurs using the advantage of their size,
E ach of the weak losing their lives.

D inosaurs roamed in the past,
I n times when pterodactyl flew extremely fast.
N ever again will they terrorise the land,
O nly because their fossils live in the sand.
S low and the feeble are all killed,
A nd the strong and speedy with stomachs filled.
U tahraptor, deadly predator, killing everything in its path,
R age and fury making him uncontrollable in his wrath.

A ll that is history now,
G reat creatures like these are as fast as the cheetah,
E very second they ran further than a metre.

Rajan Pooni (12)

Eliminate That Stereotype

Teenagers are nasty things,
Never should have been invented,
Alcoholics, street corner hogging,
Hoodies, yobs, hooligans, chavs,
Crime addicts, thieving, stealing,
Foul-mouthed, cheeky, swearing,
Aggressive, fighting, shooting, stabbing,
That's the stereotype of teenagers!

Now the truth is some teens are like this,
But many aren't, they're quite the opposite,
Sober, social, law-abiding,
Polite, caring, self-controlling,
That's what real teenagers are like.

Lee Campbell (15)
Abraham Darby School

The Chavvy Troll!

I went out in the street one day
I just went out to have a play,
We were all filled with sweet delight,
We weren't ready for this big fright.
The troll came down the street, *bang, bang, bang!*
Then he started speaking slang!
'Yo man, innit-safe to you?'
Oh my God, what shall we do?

So we decided to have some fun,
We took the micky out of his great big bum.
He was raging, anger filled his eyes but to us,
                              that was no surprise!
'Gonna tell your mother you've been dissin' me man,
You ain't no homie, you're no fam!'
We stood there giggling, hand in hand,
Then my mate drew out a rubber band,
He twanged it once, he twanged it twice,
We decided to add some musical spice.
We sang along to the beat and the troll went running back
                                    down the street.

So if you see the chavvy troll one day,
Don't be afraid to sing and play!

Natalie Newsome (12)
Idsall School

Why?

Why must we destroy our world which we all hold so dear,
As if its end is something that none of us need fear?
Why must people fight over the things that they believe?
Why do we not give, yet we demand that we receive?
Why is it we take for granted our ample food supplies,
Whilst somewhere far away someone not so lucky dies?
Of all these big questions, there is one more I will ask,
Is righting all these wrongs too impossible a task?

Alex Langton (12)
Idsall School

I Am The Girl

I am the girl who hides her feelings, she buries them deeply
and tattoos a smile to her face.
I am the girl whose friends think is happy,
always up for a laugh, hyper all the time.
I am the girl who gives advice to all her friends
I am the girl who refuses to open up to maybe receive
advice like the advice she gives to other people.
I am the girl who sees good in most people
who wouldn't always be acknowledged.
I am the girl who loves the guys though not
receiving love back.
I am the girl who doesn't give up straight away.
I am the girl who would never be considered, the girl
who's too minging or fat to ever be wanted.
I am the girl who wishes to be like her friends -
to be slim, attractive, fanciable.
I am the girl who doesn't follow fashion trends,
to wear fishnets, drainpipes or mini-skirts.
I am the girl who continues to be herself sometimes
swapping to her fake self.
I am the girl who hides her feelings, she buries them
deeply and tattoos a smile to her face.
I am the girl.

Elesia Haye (13)
Idsall School

My Book, My Mirror

My book is like a mirror . . .
reflects everything about you.
My book is like a mirror . . .
shiny, clean and new to you.
My book is like a mirror . . .
shocking like what's behind a secret door.
My book is like a mirror . . .
unpredictable but stares you right in the face.
My book is like a mirror . . .
different, every time.
My book is like a mirror . . .
Everything you want it to be!

Kim Richens (12)
Idsall School

My Poem

I walked in front, never thinking,
That soon, people's feelings would be sinking.
I took one step onto the road, not knowing.
No signs to me were showing.
A car came, I hit the ground,
Not making any sound.
My arms fell beside me,
My eyes shut, I couldn't see.
I felt my heart thump once then twice,
My life would soon depend on one dice.
Sirens were ringing in and out,
All I wanted was to call and shout.
My body felt like it was lifted,
Was this the end, as I drifted?

The music turned on in a small room,
I had just slightly missed my doom.

Eleri Newman (12)
Idsall School

Untitled

Her eyes were like little brown beads
Stuck on her face as though she was a teddy bear.
Fluffy little ears.
Little belly that you could fall asleep on.
Just sits there, as if she hasn't got a care in the world.
Eating lovely food.
Watching the blazing sunset,
Praying for another day.
Strong little legs for hanging.
Sharp nails for defending.
Short hair on her belly, as though she'd shaved.
Can change in an instant,
Cute and fluffy,
Too mean and protective,
Always stay the same Mum,
Never change.

Lauren Withers (12)
Idsall School

My Monkey

My monkey is brave
He'd do anything to save.
My monkey is cheeky,
People find him freaky.
His tail, it sways,
In different ways.
My monkey, he talks,
More than he walks.
He lounges about and watches TV,
But he goes ape whenever he sees me.
He loves his bananas
And his pyjamas.
He likes to sleep
And he likes to creep.
We play hide and go seek,
But he cheats and he peeks.
I love my little monkey,
No matter how chunky.

Rachel Sharpe (12)
Idsall School

Pegasus

Inside Pegasus' eyes, there's the flash of lightning,
Inside the flash of lightning, there's the horse's gallop.
Inside the horse's gallop, there's a ticking of a clock.
Inside the ticking clock, there's the spread of wings.
Inside the spread of wings, there's the flight of a horse.
Inside the horse's flight, there's a gust of wind,
Inside the gust of wind, there's the Pegasus' mane.
Inside the Pegasus' mane, there's the golden sun,
Inside the golden sun, there's Pegasus' eyes.

Stephanie Chan (12)
Idsall School

Snow Leopard

S wiftly he moves
N ervous of animals,
O val eyes open wide.
W ind speed, he runs.

L eaping back home,
E asy work for him,
O ver snowy rocks,
P ounding back home.
A round him, animals watch him eat.
R ipping the animals apart
D igging his sharp teeth into his head.

James Marfleet (13)
Idsall School

A Whale

This one graceful animal glides across the sea,
He threw himself to the surface as if for me to see.
This one fat, gentle animal wobbles in the ocean,
He looks drunk and drowsy as if he's drunk a potion.
This one slow-moving animal hums in the Pacific,
He screams and shouts as he goes along
As if he's hit a wicket.
This one vegetarian animal chomps in the Atlantic,
He sees a ship and gets really, really frantic.
What am I?
A whale.

Jessica Marsh (13)
Idsall School

A Cat

A cat has fluffy fur,
When it sleeps it will purr.
A cat has a long tail
It will tickle your nose, no fail.
A cat has a wet pink nose,
It also has long sharp nails.
A cat has glistening eyes
It will catch any bird that goes by.

Emma Smith (12)
Idsall School

Black Rhino

B ig and brutal, it
L umbers across
A cres of grassland
C overing plants as it
K eeps on going

R estlessly moving slowly
H ammering its ways
I n need of food
N othing would stop it.
O nwards it goes in search of food.

Sean Meade (12)
Idsall School

What Am I?

I have floppy ears.
I have large floppy ears.
I am white and have large floppy ears.
I am fluffy, white and have large floppy ears.
I am small, fluffy, white and have large floppy ears.
I am cute, small, fluffy, white and have large floppy ears.
I hop and I am cute, small, fluffy, white and have large floppy ears.
I am a rabbit!

Carys Jones (12)
Idsall School

Poem

My dad is a dragon,
My dad is big and strong like a dragon.
My dad is the best, big and strong like a dragon.
My dad has hair like scales and is the best,
and strong like a dragon.
My dad has ears like radar, hair like scales and is the best,
big and strong like a dragon.
My dad has eyes like the sun, ears like radar, hair like scales
and is the best, big and strong like a dragon.
My dad has a mouth so big, eyes like the sun,
ears like radar, hair like scales and is the best,
big and strong, like a dragon.

Jordan Bason (12)
Idsall School

Elephant Poem

They plod along the African plain where it doesn't rain.
Their tusks are quite a sight to see.
They make hunters jump with glee,
Their ears flap to keep them cool.
They also swim in a deep mud pool.
Their trunk swishes and helps them eat,
They walk to a steady beat.
They eat leaves and fruit that they see,
When they're with their herd, they're as busy as a bee,
Their skin is as rough as a log.
They are never scared of a huge wild dog,
Some are as tall as a house,
Some are scared of a mouse.

Jordan Wildsmith (12)
Idsall School

My Family

My dad is a frog
He likes to jog,
My mum is a cow
She's always saying, 'Wow!'
My sister's a baboon
She plays with the spoons,
My brother is a mouse
He always hides in the house.
My nan is a pig
She wears a wig,
My grandad is a bear
He eats lots of pears.
My aunty is a whale
She loves to sail
My uncle is a woodlouse
But he's as big as a house.
My teacher asked us to bring a pet to school
But I can't bring my pets,
They aren't cool.
Just bring them in
I can't win cos they're my family.

Alexandra Whitear (12)
Idsall School

Untitled

There once was a dragon who lived high
on the mountain, a big scary dragon he was,
his red scales running all over.

His wings were a shadowy black colour
with a few gold spots.
Whenever he went hunting, he would
always come back with an animal or a human.

His wings would stretch out as far as they could go,
then with one strong push he lifts into the air
carrying with him the prey of the night.

Jamie Buclaw (12)
Idsall School

Snakes

I am a snake
A very harmful snake
You will see me slithering
I will be dithering
You won't know I'm there
I can eat a hare.

I am a ticking time bomb
I will kill you and your mum
Tick, tick, tick . . . boom!

Sakir Hussain (12)
Idsall School

Confused Cow!

There was a cow, who was confused,
He baa'd and baa'd but never mooed.
The other cows, they thought him odd,
The birds above would grin and nod.
He ached to be all fluffy and cute,
Instead he thought he was a brute.

There was a cow who was confused,
He oinked and oinked but never mooed.
He longed to roll around in mud,
He wished and wished and wished he could.
He yearned to have a curly tail,
What did he do? Weep and wail.

There was a cow who was confused,
He clucked and clucked but never mooed.
He craved to lay a chicken's egg,
All he could do was wait and beg.
He wished to have a feathered coat,
The finest hens would strut and gloat.

There was a cow who understood,
Who mooed and mooed as best he could.
He lay and chewed green grass all day,
He didn't need to stay away.
From the others in the herd,
As they no longer thought him absurd.

Jess Bowrin (12)
Idsall School

A Nightmare Come True

I remember the words of my grandad
Walking in the room
All of a sudden he dropped back down
Out with a great boom
Screams, tantrums, tears
This can't be happening
These are my greatest fears.
To the hospital he went
All the thoughts that it was his time
I didn't think it was meant
The phone rang, my heart skipped a beat.
I couldn't stand up
I felt that I had no feet.
The news came, he was sadly dead
But I know he's always with me in my heart and my head.

Yasmen Holyday (12)
Idsall School

The Gremlin Behind My Bedroom Cupboard

Behind my bedroom cupboard
Not known to anyone but me
There's a little gremlin
With the name of Bertie
He comes out in the dead of night
When I am fast asleep
And messes up my tidy room so it looks like a heap
He pulls out all the drawers
He takes the picture off the walls
He scatters CDs all around
Clothes piled high in a mound
The floor is covered with bits and bobs
Gives me lots of cleaning jobs
Dirty socks everywhere
So it made my mother stop and stare
And ask me what the hell I'd done
I answered with some cheeky pun
'It wasn't me who made this dirty,
It was my gremlin with the name of Bertie.'
'Young lady, mind your cheek
You are grounded for one whole week!'

Charlie Harper (13)
Idsall School

Summer Of '98

I take you back to 1998,
In Ibiza, summer holiday resort.
Where a little girl the age of four sat with the Thomson crew.
When she ran away and wasn't caught.
Down the hot beach,
It seems like miles and miles.
She didn't want to be taught,
How to throw a stupid volleyball.
Into the hotel, slip across the marble,
And try and reach the button in the lift.
Up and up, she was reaching the end up to the room,
Where it was going to be doom.
Three, two, one blackout!

Cerys Thomas (12)
Idsall School

The Big Bang

The sweet sound of silence
The sweet scent of awe
Looking into the emptiness
It felt oh such a bore

Suddenly something amazing happened,
Upon that wonderful scene,
An explosion of the galaxies
The planet and stars had been

The Big Bang they call it
It happened many years ago
If anyone else were to have seen it
They would be filled full of wow!

But I was there at that magical sight
And that's my story to tell
A huge explosion up in space
Now the Earth works oh so well.

Courtney Fudge (12)
Idsall School

The Sky!

The sky is a motorway,
filled with fluffy pillows and
jammed with feather-winged fish.
With great giant cars zooming past,
towards the huge orange tunnel to pass through time,
when the motorway drops dark the giant cars
re-appear through a white passageway.

Many other cars are flashing their lights,
we see them, tiny white dots, flickering in the distance.
What wonderful sights.

We seem like ants on the ground, compared to the
giant cars, zooming around.
Children fly their kites and watch the feathered fish
fly at different heights!
The sky is a motorway filled with fluffy pillows
and jammed with feather-winged fish.
The never-ending motorway, the sky.
Imagine the traffic!

Kimberley Easthope (13)
Idsall School

Monkey Knows All!

I was sprawled across our old sofa, watching the TV,
Suddenly a monkey walked in, or was it a chimpanzee?
He said, 'What are you doing here, sat so miserably?'
I answered, 'I don't know what you mean,
I'm actually quite happy.'

'How can you be so happy while stuck in a place like this?'
'You need to be outside in the fresh air that you've missed.'
'What fresh air, I hear you say, I don't see any here?'
'The clean crisp air that waits outside, it's been there years and years.'

Rachael Moreland (12)
Idsall School

Seeing Is Believing

Seeing trees swaying in the breeze on the hilltops,
with their leaves of gold, emerald and ruby,
glittering from the dew.
Seeing different people in different clothing,
with the colours dancing around in the street.
Seeing birds flying in the sky,
looking like smudges of all colours.
Seeing is believing, always know so,
everything you see is part of your life.

Francesca White **(12)**
Idsall School

Shivers

Creeping like a sleek, sly vixen,
The arduous, grating winter sets in.
Autumn shades die, replaced by crisp,
New bed sheets of white.

> And the bare trees shiver in the
> Bleak, bitter breeze.
> Hark the shrewd birds flying south.

Sleeping cosily, wrapped up warm
The haunting whistle outside the window.
An open fire ablaze with the pungent smell of pine
Wafting throughout the home;

> And the bare trees shiver in the
> Bleak, bitter breeze.
> Hark the shrewd birds flying south.

Lucy Burden (12)
Idsall School

At The Bottom Of My Garden

There is a little fairy at the bottom of my garden
She sings and dances and smiles
She lives in a flower pot wonderland
With magic all around
Oh she can do such magic with a wave of her wand
That creates such sparks and sounds
She can make a cupboard full of cookies
Quicker than you'd think and
The fabrics from her clothes are beautifully exquisite
Woven gold, silk and silver
Lace, brocade and velvet
But the secret to her magic is
That she leaves a sprinkle of fairy dust
On whatever she composes
There was a little fairy at the bottom of my garden
But now she has left to do better things
Although whenever I eat a cookie or see a dress of gold
I think about the fairy that lived
At the bottom of my garden.

Nicholl Heath (12)
Idsall School

Life

Life is irreplaceable, life is great.
No one deserves a terrible fate.
It is to be treasured as a wonderful thing,
Nobody knows who the Lord will bring.

Most people live and die very calm,
After all, there is no need to be alarmed.
They have lived and done what they can
And followed in the footsteps of Man.

A lot of people grow up and get married,
They have a baby, who is carried
Through its life until it can look after itself.
Then it will work for its own wealth.

Some people deal with life very well,
But some end up going to Hell!
Just don't waste a second of your time,
You've got to admit this is a pretty good rhyme.

Shahin Jogi (12)
Idsall School

Love

Love is a fire
Within someone's heart
Frozen when you're lonely.

Love is a tightrope
You can keep your balance
Or fall off and not get helped back.

Love is happiness
Full of laughs
And good times.

Love is a feeling of affection
For a person
Or an item.

Love is sorrow
When you can't see
The person you like.

Love is hate
When you give someone your heart
And they thrust it back.

Love is time
It seems to drag
When you're not with your loved one.

Hannah Davis (12)
Idsall School

I Am Like . . .

I am like a mountain bike, racing over all the bumps
and obstacles of life.
I am like a meerkat, watching my surroundings and
taking them in.
I am like tuna sandwiches, a boring white outside
but inside
I am friendly and nice.
I am like a dandelion, I blend into stuff,
I'm common but sometimes stand out
and in your face.

Matthew Norton (12)
Idsall School

Weather - When God Is

Weather is like emotions,
When God is proud,
It is beaming, sizzling and calm.
When God is mischievous,
It is moist, miserable and treacherous.
When God is excited,
It is short, sharp and blazing.
When God is interrogated,
It is misty, mysterious and gloomy.

When God is . . .

Nathan Le-Moine (12)
Idsall School

My School Poem

My school is a prison
Cramped children chained in a cell.
The bell rings and the doors open,
The children get beat and choken.
The bell rings again, it's time for class.
And near the doors is a big mass.
All the inmates are wishing and hoping.
They could all go home.

Jack Peters (14)
Idsall School

A Photo

A photo is just a photo
It can be tall
It can be small
It may have lots of people in it.
It may have none at all.
Could have animals in it
Or could just have nothing
Or could be a blur.

Kirsty Arscott (13)
Idsall School

I Am What I Am

I am what I am
Don't try to change me
I will never be your masterpiece
So don't bother
I am what I am

I have memories of the good
Also the bad
I don't see the point now
Of worrying about the past
It is what it is
And you can't change that

Sometimes things go my way
But often they don't
But it doesn't bother me
I am what I am

I know I have friends I can trust
Yet I know whom I don't
That is not a problem
I am what I am

Sometimes I feel nervous
Just like everyone else
And this makes me what I am!

Kate Watton (13)
Idsall School

Ode To The Lawnmower

Please accept that it's not my fault that I have been named
a Suffolk Colt.
All winter long I wait to hear the sound of the screeching gate.
Then the gate will let me through because I have a job to do.
Pull my cord to start me up with a splutter and a hiccup.
When the neighbours hear my roar they soon come knocking
on my door.
My piston races up and down, as I crawl across the ground.
With my name up on my side, the lawn I mow with all my pride.
Up and down the lawn I go, cutting grass as I mow,
As my blade rotates around, it cuts the weeds down to the ground.
The cuttings shower right through the air, into the grass by
sitting there.
Soon the lawn is looking trim as the grass box fills to the brim.
Very soon I am put away, ready for another day.

Oliver Vincent (13)
Idsall School

The Killer

His eyes were burning flames
His scales were like armour
His tail like a whip
He burnt a soldier to the ground
He smashed his way through gates
He swallowed a man along with his horse
Only to die minutes later.

Andy Lee (12)
Idsall School

Bully, Bully, Please Go Away!

Bully, bully,
Please go away,
You're making me scared,
He said, 'No way!'

He gets me into trouble
By pretending it was me,
I know I didn't do it,
So why can't people see?

I really cannot take it,
They make me want to die,
I'm going bit by bit,
I'm going to say goodbye.

Camila Burns-Roa (13)
Idsall School

The Zoo

My school is a zoo.
Temperature's mainly mild,
Animals always wild.
Zookeepers lose control.
Children, very annoying,
They drive me up the wall,
Always screaming, shouting, pointing.
If only they knew the phrase 'silence is golden'.
This is why you need to
Get me out of here!

Adam Chell (13)
Idsall School

When I Was Five

I remember when I was five,
Having the time of my life,
I just kept on walking along,
Listening to the waves making a song.
As I started to dig,
I saw people playing tig.
I dug, dug, dug, dug, dug,
Until I felt a slight tug.
I turned around, saw a familiar face and gave her a hug.
I showed my mom the hole I had dug
And we went back taking small paces,
Returning back towards my base.

Simon Chell (13)
Idsall School

My Poem

The school is a jungle
    Living creatures learning
        Deathly people looking over you
          Never-ending journey
      Hot, humid, god, so boring!
    All the trees getting in my way,
I'm a pupil get me outta here.

Alex Nicholas (13)
Idsall School

The Court

The court is a body!
It is full of small curious cells digging for the truth.
The judge is the strength, firm, understanding, yet always
standing tall.
Yet the walls know all with their eyes so cruel.
Beware, the court knows all.

Laurence Riley (13)
Idsall School

Toy Soldier Camp

My school is a camp of toy soldiers,
completely controlled by a greater force.
Soldiers march from place to place,
dressed in identical uniform with no smile on their face.
But they all keep their equipment cased,
because every so often they get a chance to leave,
they go into the field with information to retrieve,
to go back to camp to be disciplined and to learn.

Matthew Pollard (13)
Idsall School

My School

My school is like a town centre,
Shops you like, shops you hate,
People telling you where to go,
Shops are different colours, you get confused,
You can always hear music,
It never leaves your side.

My school is like a motorway,
Big cars, small cars, running at different speeds,
Driver telling wheels what to do,
Different noises all the time,
Where can I go?
What should I do?

My school is like a book,
You have to get into it before you can judge it,
Characters you like, characters you hate,
The hustle and bustle of different activities,
Different scenarios all the time.

My school raises me up so high,
But yet, it still makes me sigh!

Suzanne Turner (13)
Idsall School

My School

My school is a warzone
Chaos at every corner
Noises shoot around
There is never peace
I do just wish
I could just leave it all behind me
We are all privates in this army
Please don't remind me
But those who are in command
Control every little thing
I just wish I could go
Go to that sunny place
Where there is no chaos
And finally
Finally I am at peace.

Americk Pamma (13)
Idsall School

Is That The Castle?

Is that the castle built on a steep hill in the middle of nowhere
                                    with waves of fog hugging it?
Is that the castle with the most ghost sightings in the world?
Is that the castle where many people go in but are never seen again?
Is that the castle covered in creepy cobwebs made by
                                    a monstrous spider army?
Is that the castle that is supposedly the entrance to Hell?
I don't know but I'm going to find out!

Benedict Leader (11)
Idsall School

Night

The sun disappears behind the horizon,
Out comes the moon and beams down its reflective light.
Owls hoot as bats stir.
Crickets sing,
Their legs rubbing in time.
Owls hoot more,
As they swiftly peer out of their nest.
Is the coast clear?
What's for tea tonight?
All of the creatures think.
More stir.
The night is alive with a thousand creatures.
Noisy, so noisy.
So many different sounds to be heard.
Crickets, flies, mosquitoes and still many more.
More hunt and battle for the best prey.
As it gets warmer, they know they'll have to make do with
The food they've got.
The sun's rays appear and all is silent,
As the first human wakes.

Frances Lacey (11)
Idsall School

Invisible

Here I am,
Alone in the void,
With no one to talk to,
No one,
I am not invisible,
So why am I not here?

I always have my hands up,
In class,
But even the teachers
Act like I'm not there,
I always do good work,

I looked at myself today
And saw my hand was gone,
Me being ignored,
Had turned me into a girl who was invisible,

No one noticed that I am slowly disappearing,
Disappearing,
I walk around as I slowly not become in this world,
A scream . . .

I existed no longer in this world of pain . . .

Verity Louise Harris (11)
Idsall School

My Dog Finley

When I come home I know that he will always be there
And never let me down
I can talk to him about anything
And he will never laugh
Or call me stupid
And I know he will always like me
No matter how I dress
Or how my hair looks
And his tail is always wagging
And he looks at me like I'm the best person in the world
And he's so pretty
And I love him lots and lots and lots.

Emma Simpson (12)
Idsall School

I Have A Dream

I'm now on a shelf where nobody looks,
I feel out of place with these new modern books,
I'm dusty and I have a broken spine,
But my insides are so divine,
I know I'm covered in cobwebs and coffee
And some of my pages are stuck together with toffee,

But I have a dream . . .

You see the secret of me,
Is I hold fairy tales, couldn't you see,
Girls with long hair and frilly white dresses,
Wicked old witches who conjure up messes,

In my dream, I will be picked
And somebody will read my script.

Emily Hughes (11)
Newport Girls' High School

A Thousand For Peace

I have a dream that one day
The people of the world
Unite as one

No matter where
No matter when

Strangers across the globe
Don't pass unnoticed in the street
They turn and smile
Wave a friendly 'hello'

Broken families come together
To forget their past
And embrace their future

The old man
That sleeps on the park bench
Is welcomed warmly into homes
Accepted as an important part
Of our community

Different races, religions
Stop fighting wars
And sing songs
Of praise and hope
To their children
And their children's children

A thousand flowers line the streets
A sign of peace and joy
To all

I have a dream that one day
The people of the world
Unite as one

Let's do it.

Alice Roman (14)
Newport Girls' High School

I Have A Dream

I have a dream that I will climb the highest mountain,
That I will swim deep in the sea.
I have a dream that I will fly south with the birds in winter
And that the angels will never come to take me . . .

. . . But I'm lying here now, on my deathbed, weak,
91 years old, gaunt, tired and pale
As the endless days pass me by
All I can do is dream, so hopeless and frail.

I dream that I will walk to the South Pole,
That I will hunt with the lions for prey.
I dream that I am an Indian prince riding an elephant
And that I will never have to face Judgement Day . . .

. . . But these are just dreams, I'm in a reality
My life has been wasted here in the UK,
I should have travelled and explored the world,
I'll die as a nobody and will be left to decay.

I dream that I am a ranger roaming the rainforest
Or a performer up on that stage.
I dream that I will live forever
And that I will never die of old age.

My time is up, it's hard to breathe,
My family and friends gather around,
I say my last words then close my eyes,
My feelings right now are so profound.

I see a bright light, I'm at the gates,
I'm let in, 'Oh joy,' not a long wait.
I look around and soon can see
Heaven's much better than any dream could ever be.

Hannah Partridge (13)
Newport Girls' High School

I Had A Dream

(Based on the speech by Martin Luther King)

I had a dream
Which changed the Earth,
I gave life
To a new beginning
Where black and white
Shared a world
Together in arms.
Brothers.

Peace is final,
Wars are over,
Lost at last
Is discrimination.
Away from us
Our shared land,
Side by side.
Partners.

We were soldiers,
Peace was our goal,
We obtained
Our conclusive mission.
Now we stand strong
With each soul
United on taunt.
True friends.

I had a dream
And it came true.
Once that was
Just imaginary,
Is now all real.
Now the world
Can live in peace.
As one.

Samantha Brizuela (14)
Newport Girls' High School

Passing Identities

I stroll up the street,
Passing you by.
Just another nameless identity
In a faceless crowd.

Our eyes meet, a second in a lifetime,
Suggestion of colour?
Just another nameless identity
In a faceless crowd . . .

I could have long hair and you, short.
A highly paid job and good qualifications,
But I'm still
Just another nameless identity
In a faceless crowd.

I wonder if you're clever,
I ponder if you're kind.
Even though you're
Just another nameless identity
In a faceless crowd.

I am, he is, you are.
'The characteristics, that make
You who you are?'
Still,
Just another nameless identity
In a faceless crowd.

I can't picture your face anymore.
After all, it was only a few seconds,
A brief meeting in the eye of time.
Yet
Just another nameless identity
In a faceless crowd . . .

Knowing, finding,
Judging and deciding.
Classifications, unique personality?
I may never see you again,
But I will remember
The other nameless identity
In that faceless crowd.

Camilla Crawshaw (16)
Newport Girls' High School

I Have A Dream

I had a dream about a fantastic day at school last night

H aving gotten everything right I was feeling happy
A mazingly I found my way round easily
V ery exciting I know
E verything hard became easy-peasy

A rt was a doddle

D oing chemistry was really fun
R eally scrumptious lunch today too
E verything was really super
A ctually it was better than that
M mm, yes I had a dream about a fantastic day at school last night.

Harriet Boxley (11)
Newport Girls' High School

I Have A Dream . . .

I have a dream
Of a world of no pain,
Never will we fail,
Only gain.

I have a dream
Of a world with peace,
Anger will be gone
And danger will cease.

I have a dream,
Disease will be gone,
Illness is forgotten,
Dying will be none.

If I wish hard enough,
My dreams might come true.

I have a dream,
Do you?

Hannah Mitchell (11)
Newport Girls' High School

I Have A Dream

I have a dream of a world full of kindness
And loads of happiness to spare
And love and generosity
In everyone, everywhere.
I dream of laughter and fairness,
No more poverty or starving children
And everyone to be friendly.
No more cruelty to animals or children,
But I know it should be impossible to exist.

Alice Moreton (11)
Newport Girls' High School

I Dreamt I Had A Baby

I dreamt I had a baby,
I was in the baby's mind.
I sensed its first look,
Into a world of humankind.

Its first smell was of blood,
Death and cruelty,
Hate and revenge,
Torture and evil.
Its first smell was not good.

Its first sight was of love,
Happiness and loyalty,
Kindness and sensitivity,
Sharing and giving.
Its first sight gave it peace as does a dove.

Its first sounds were of talking,
Of calamity and murder but,
Help and teaching,
Liking and loving.
Its first sounds got it thinking.

It looked further still
And took a big decision,
Good over evil,
Or evil over good.

It took its first breath -
And screamed.

Jenny Rowe (11)
Newport Girls' High School

I Have A Dream

I have a dream when I fall asleep
Of flowers dancing in the sun,
Of woodland creatures skipping across the forest floor,
Of mice tucking baby mice into their thumb-sized cradles,
Of fairies sheltering under toadstools,
Of all the world being bright and cheerful,
Of all the people being friends.
Then I wake up,
The next night I have a dream,
The flowers are lying dead under dark clouds,
The woodland creatures are nowhere to be seen,
The mummy mice were never there and the baby mice are not born,
The toadstools have been stamped on and fairies don't exist,
The world isn't visible, the darkness is too black,
The people never speak and there are fights around the street.
Then I wake up
And realise I can make a difference,
I can have a *dream!*

Eleanor Lane (12)
Newport Girls' High School

Unanswerable Questions

The rope of love strangles me as I spill into the world,
Unconditional love for all, write my name on the wall,
I promise to catch you if you ever should fall.
Listen, as my tale of existence is unfurled,
Watch, as my fragile body is hurled
Into the chaos of life and I call
Upon all my power to make a difference for all
And bring joy, forgiveness and meaning to the world.

Am I a parasite? Is it worth struggling through birth?
Are we an alien's experiment gone wrong, a game or a dream?
Are we the best or the worst mistake ever made on Earth?
Am I an illusion, is it real when I scream?
Am I a pink, useless lump of flesh?
Don't tell me I'm nature's way of keeping meat fresh.

Heather Clarke (17)
Newport Girls' High School

Flowers

F uchsia, pink as a piglet
L avender, purple as a plum
O rchid, so many colours like a rainbow
W aterlillies, white as snow
E lder flower to make some lovely wine
R oses, red as deep love
S o that's my poem, do you like it?

Jessica Bellingham (11)
Rhyn Park School & Performing Arts College

Trixie

H is for the hay Trixie eats
O is for the oats, her favourite treat
R is for reins, which you hold on tight
S is for saddle, which you sit upon
E is for eating which she loves to do!

Jess Austin
Rhyn Park School & Performing Arts College

Peace!

Peace is a snow-white swan swifting on sparkling spring water,
Peace is like a dove flying in the air,
Peace is like dolphins jumping out the sea,
Peace is like a mouse who creeps throughout his home,
Peace is everywhere, on the ground and in the air
But we just cannot see it,
Peace is a group of people sharing their love and friendship.

Elle Hughes (11)
Rhyn Park School & Performing Arts College

World War!

The bell just went.
Time to go underground.
The Germans coming over.
They see any light, they will drop their bombs.
English men trying to kill the Germans.
Germans on the top of London.
We hope they will not drop those bombs.
I hear a bomb being dropped.
It's coming shooting down.
It's like thunder.
Bang! It dropped. I hope that was not a house.
The bell just went, time to come back up.
All I see is the fire getting higher and higher.
I hope this stops now before it's too late.

Bradley Coombes (11)
Rhyn Park School & Performing Arts College

Seasons

In spring as a lamb skips by,
Frolicking softly like a butterfly,
As summer comes the sun shines bright,
A short gentle walk, as the moths come out at night.
Summer ends, autumn draws nigh,
Rain dampens the ground, fireworks light up the sky.
Winter's here, get ready for snow,
What is that? Santa, ho, ho, ho!

Ashleigh Birks (11)
Rhyn Park School & Performing Arts College

Subjects

Geography teaches you from England to Spain.
Geography is all about weather like the sun and the rain.

Science teaches you from water to chemicals.
Science is all about poison like mercury.

English teaches you from stories to poems.
English is all about reading and writing.

Maths teaches you from numbers to algebra.
Maths is all about multiplications like five and ten.

Gareth Jones (11)
Rhyn Park School & Performing Arts College

The Next World

Have you ever wondered where people go
When they have passed away?
This is what really happens . . .

You get sent up through the clouds,
Drifting, drifting,
Above the clouds, above the stars,
There's a place exactly the opposite . . .

Where all the pigs fly
And all the cows talk,
The humans all moo
And babies are brought by storks.
The adults go *goo ga*
And the boys wear girls' clothes,
The teachers misbehave
And in class time have a doze.

So now you've heard about the next world,
Are you sure you want to go?
Have a little think and next time
Let me know!

Carlee Louise Hands (11)
Rhyn Park School & Performing Arts College

Bird

I wonder what it would be like to be a bird,
To be able to fly free up in the sky,
Never knowing where the wind flow will take me,
Never knowing what I may see.

Going over hills and mountains and out to sea,
Always watching your back for bigger birds and cats,
Always on the lookout for something nice to eat.
I am sure there is nothing nicer than to fly free in the sky,
Never having to see a teacher but only from the sky,
But if you have a good aim you can get them in the eye!

Daniel Whittall
Rhyn Park School & Performing Arts College

If I Was An Animal

If I was a lion
I would roar all day
It would sound like a generator

If I was a snake
I would hiss all through the night
It would sound like wind blowing through the trees

If I was a monkey
I would swing from tree to tree
It would look like a pendulum

If I was a horse
I would make loud noises all day
It would be as noisy as a firework

If I was a parrot
I would talk all day
It would sound like a chatterbox

If I was a tortoise
I would walk slowly all day
It would look like a slow Fert 500.

Luke Wotton (11)
Rhyn Park School & Performing Arts College

Untitled

I am a bike too fast to see
Can you guess what I am?
I'm a Kawasaki
Too fast for the eye of a human
Too fast for the eye of a cat
I look like a heap of metal
Stuck together by a bat
I have grips that people grasp
To turn me around corners.

Zac Martin
Rhyn Park School & Performing Arts College

Guess What I Am . . .

I am an animal in the sky flying high.
I have brown and black fur.
I've got wings and feathers.
I collect twigs to make a nest.
I eat worms and chips.
I poo in people's eyes.
Guess what I am . . .
I'm a bird.

Jessica Birch (11)
Rhyn Park School & Performing Arts College

Cars

Whilst a Ferrari drives round the mountains,
A little boy plays in the fountains.

Whilst you watch a race car drift round a corner,
I think you would rather be in a sauna.

When you see the driver of the Lamborghini,
I bet you're thinking . . . *nice beasty.*

When you see the Bugatti go 200 miles per hour,
You notice that on the road it crushes a flower.

Now that this is the end of the poem,
I think I would rather go back to my house in Gobowen.

Grant John Drury (11)
Rhyn Park School & Performing Arts College

I Wish I Was Johnny Depp

I wish I was Johnny Depp because he gets
A ton of money from movies
All the beautiful ladies he wants
Expensive supercars and huge mansions
And on set, the Caribbean scenery
An awarding feature film.

James Griffiths (11)
Rhyn Park School & Performing Arts College

My Kittens

I have two kittens in my house,
They like to play with their mouse.

When I walk they grab my toes
And they like to paw my nose.

One is ginger,
One is white.

George and Chester,
They love to fight.

One is fat and one is thin,
They use the cat flap to get in.

They sleep all night and play all day,
They even chase the dog away.

They bite my shoes, they bite my slippers,
They go mad when we have kippers.

I love my kittens, they're really ace,
I'm glad they live at my place.

Ryan Gibson (12)
Rhyn Park School & Performing Arts College

I Wish . . .

I wish I was a pussycat flying through the sky,
Where I could see everything with a glance of my big eye.

I wish I was a dog guarding like a hound,
If anyone should come near me I'd knock them to the ground.

I wish I was a superhero fighting crime all day,
If anyone commits a crime they wouldn't get away.

But most of all I just wish I could be me,
Sitting down all day and being lazy.

Michael Evans (12)
Rhyn Park School & Performing Arts College

Football

Football is the love of my life,
Or could it be my mother?
Orange at half-time,
The ref blew his whistle.
Bewildered that it was offside
And we could have won the game.
Now I'm lying in my bed,
That was not a dream.
It was a nightmare.

Kieran Evans (12)
Rhyn Park School & Performing Arts College

Free

What is free?
Where is free?

Somewhere safe,
Where people care,
Somewhere equal,
Where slaves aren't there.

Is free a place with
No more whippings and no more rags
And no more torture to make us sad?

To get to freedom I must believe
That I am worthy and I am free.

What is free?
Free will be me.

Where is free?
Free is Canada.

Sally Beddow (11)
Rhyn Park School & Performing Arts College

Balloon

Stop stretching me, it hurts,
Pulling me this way and that.

Oh no now you're putting your garlicky breath into me.

Help I'm stretching, I don't want to be fat,
Surely you're out of breath by now.

Now they're trying to twist my neck into a knot
Eek eek, I can't breathe.

They're letting me go, I'm floating,
I'm free, free, free from the garlic,
The hot breath, the knots and *argh - pigeon!*

Caitlin Roberts (11)
Rhyn Park School & Performing Arts College

Lost

Lost . . .
She's gone
Lost . . .
My best friend lost forever or so it seems
Lost . . .
No other friends
Lost . . .
I have no life without her
Lost . . .
She's gone to live away
Lost . . .
My best friend moved away.

Hannah Jones (11)
Rhyn Park School & Performing Arts College

Summer

The summer sun in the sky,
The bluebell flowers rising high!
Filling up the paddling pool,
Jumping in and being cool.

Making fresh lemonade
For the family to slurp away,
A healthy salad we like to crunch,
That's what we have for our lunch.

A picnic basket full of food,
Sitting by the riverside,
I feel so relaxed right now,
Too bad summer can't last.

Lucy Minter (11)
Rhyn Park School & Performing Arts College

Peace

I used to be happy
But not anymore
Life doesn't seem fair
Now my family's life all seems to be bare
The weather was bad
I was at risk leaving them sad
As I lay there dead
My family cry in their beds
And so I lay down to sleep
I leave my family to weep
Although I am not gone
I will follow them from beyond
As I watch from the sky
It's never time to say goodbye.

Jade Wickenden (11)
Rhyn Park School & Performing Arts College

War Child

I was put on a train
And sent far away,
To a place I did not know
And I did not want to go,
With my gas mask and case
And a very sad face,
Then the station master's whistle did blow.

I stayed on a farm,
Where I came to no harm,
As the bombs were dropped on the city,
I made a new friend called Kitty,
When I went home at the end of the war,
To leave her it was such a pity.

Chloe Roberts (12)
Rhyn Park School & Performing Arts College

Things I Like

My dog Cherry,
She follows me and licks me lots.

My friends
Because, when I am lonely, they come and play.

My school,
Because I learn different subjects.
My teachers,
Sometimes they make me laugh.

Dinosaurs,
Some eat people, some don't.
They move in different ways,
Eat different things.

Sophie Knight (11)
Rhyn Park School & Performing Arts College

The Changing Seasons

Spring

Spring brings the animals, the buds, the leaves and sun,
The lambs in the field play and have fun.

Summer

Summer brings the warmth and holidays by the sea,
There's a busy day ahead for the pollen bee.

Autumn

Fruit starts to ripen and will eventually fall,
Fruits of all colours, varieties, large and small . . .
Acorns, conkers and colourful leaves,
Falling in the cool swirling breeze.
Raking leaves and seeds dispersing,
Hallowe'en coming and bonfires burning.

Winter

Winter brings forth the ice and snow,
Christmas is coming and snowflakes blow.
Hibernating animals are cosy in their dens,
They are watching for spring to come around again.

Rosie Evans (11)
Rhyn Park School & Performing Arts College

Aliens

If I could do anything unrealistic, I would see some . . .

A bducted to another dimension
L ittle aliens, big aliens and more
I magine an alien at home
E ver tried alien beef soup?
N othing like alien lemonade
S illy aliens, crazy aliens and mad ones.

Selina Ellis (11)
Rhyn Park School & Performing Arts College

Chocolate So Sweet

My nan is Greek, she is so sweet
She buys me chocolate so I can eat
Chocolate, chocolate that I love to eat
Makes me hyper so I don't go to sleep
Chocolate, chocolate is so sweet.

Rebecca Adams (11)
Rhyn Park School & Performing Arts College

I Can't Write A Poem

I can't really write a poem,
But believe me, I do know 'em.
I'm running out of ink
And all I've got left is pink,
So this is the end of my poem.

Matthew Henderson (11)
Rhyn Park School & Performing Arts College

Farming

F arming is the thing for me

A nimals I love, especially cows

R ounding all the animals up is for me

M ilking time is best

I n and out of the house every day

N ever stop doing jobs

G oing on the farm is the thing don't you think?

Adam Thomas (12)
Rhyn Park School & Performing Arts College

I Have . . .

I've felt the breath of the biting cold air
I've taken risks in despair
I've wished upon a glowing star
Somehow believing a wish would come from afar
I've stupidly made some mistakes
I've had my fair share of heartbreaks
I've felt the cold blow of rejection
I've been in love and offered protection
I've been young and fancy-free
I've seen all there is to see
I'm now waiting for my time to come
I'm sitting in this old battered chair
Yet why does no one seem to care?

Eleanor Hughes (14)
The Mary Webb School

Day After Day

All I ever heard was the screaming and wailing of soldiers, now dead,
It was a miserable life, on meagre rations we were fed.
Day after day, dead bodies lying all around,
All we did was sleep, eat and shoot, never a time with no sound.
We did not have the comfort of proper cosy beds,
Just soggy lumps of earth to rest our tired heads.
Day after day, the only friends we had were photographs,
We were always lonely and sad, four years with no laughs.
Day after day, hundreds, thousands of lives were lost,
How many more lives would that dreadful war cost?
Our boots were always squelching and splashing in the mud,
There was not a blade of grass,
No room for even a single flower to bud.
Day after day we could only whisper in case the enemy heard,
Why were we doing this? It just seemed absurd.
We spent mile after mile, trudging along, stamping in the soil,
The days were so long, it was an endless toil.
We missed our families greatly, but no letters could we send,
I often wondered, will this terrible war ever end?

Jack Titley (14)
The Mary Webb School

Sounds Of World War I

Shells and gunfire rattle overhead,
'Hold the line!' is what the sergeant said.
Tanks rumble across the cratered plain,
Our huge assaults have all been in vain.

Squelch go our feet in these overcrowded trenches,
Crack go our guns, when we fire at the enemy.
Boom go the tank shells as they smash into our camp,
Patter go the rain as it falls onto the ground.

Many men have been killed in this war,
'What is the point?' I ask more and more.
First Tommy Jones, then Bobby Smith was lost,
How many lives will this evil war cost?

Stutter go the machine guns, firing at our trench,
Shuffle go our feet as we move around at night.
Swoosh go our fighter planes as they fly overhead.
Clash go our bayonets as we lock in combat.

Richard Nicholson (14)
The Mary Webb School

Teenage Life!

Teenage life, a hard and struggling stage,
Teenage life, full of violence and rage.
Colour of skin making a difference isn't right,
Choice of religion causing a worldwide fight.
Walking to school with homeless on the street,
Having to be careful about people who you meet.
Young children turning to alcohol and drugs,
Then turning into violent young thugs.
Beating up people for something they need,
How will this help them succeed?
Ruining lives, not just their own,
In prison before 18, their lives they've thrown.
Teenage life, a hard and struggling stage,
Teenage life, full of violence and rage.

Amy Betton (15)
The Mary Webb School

As I Sit Here In My Doorway

As I sit here in my doorway,
The world is as cold as ice.

As I sit here in my doorway,
My stomach growls with hunger and fear.

As I sit here in my doorway,
A shiver runs through my body.

As I sit here in my doorway,
The worries of daily life lie heavy on my heart.

As I sit here in my doorway,
People pass, but no one cares.

As I sit here in my doorway,
I wonder,
When will it all end?

Amy Finnigan (14)
The Mary Webb School

Through The Eyes Of An Abandoned Animal

The dark, the cold, I try to be brave,
I'm suffering, I'm frightened, will this be my grave?

I feel betrayed and lonely, I scream and yelp,
There's silence, no one will come and help.

I wriggle and squirm, I curl up and cry,
Am I going to be left here, all alone to die?

Jan Ashley (15)
The Mary Webb School

How Do I Feel?

No one knows how I feel inside
Don't show feelings - too much pride

Although stuck in a rut
I still hide and lock it up

Like a treasure chest
Assuming it's for the best

I'm cheerful and smile
Just for a while

Till I'm all alone
With no one to phone

I just fade away
To arise the next day

I pretend nothing occurred
Do I really believe this? How absurd

Yet not a sin
To put my feelings in the bin

Just happens day in day out
Must not shout

How do I feel? I don't know
Will these feelings ever go?

Bess Robson (14)
The Mary Webb School

Through The Eyes Of Granny

Locked away in a pitch-black mind,
She'll never see the light of day,
If only once, she may,
See me looking back her way.

Having nine operations,
I wonder what it's like,
Never able to recover,
Just to get on with life.

Of all the things she tries to find,
She'll never once find me,
One split second is all it takes,
Just so she can see.

Molly Sullivan (14)
The Mary Webb School

Consequences

Standing all alone on the playground.
See the children as you look around.
They are walking towards you,
Chanting in their groups of two,
'Fat, fat, fatty.'

You walk alone,
On the way home.
Too scared to catch the bus,
In case they make a fuss.

Mum prepares your meal,
You eat it but do not reveal
That it will leave your gut
With your fingers stuck
Down your throat
You are uplifting a boat.

This goes on and on forever,
You are as delicate as a feather.
Just a year away,
They no longer say,
'Fat, fat, fatty,'
But, 'Sorry, sorry, sorry.'

Karla Giles (14)
The Mary Webb School

Grandad

He sits through the day
Watching life pass him by,
John's not getting better
And no one knows why.

He's endured operations
His memory's got worse,
I can't understand
What gave him this curse.

My grandad was active
A happy old chap,
But since he's had cancer
His old life's not back.

Eleven years on
He's deteriorating,
There isn't a cure
So for him it's frustrating.

He's fought off five strokes
And in all he's succeeded,
We've all tried our best
With support that he's needed.

But if I was to be
In his shoes for a week,
I think I'd find out
That his future is bleak.

As now I have figured
It's hard being him,
Being encaged
In an old person's skin.

Abbie Sylvester (14)
The Mary Webb School

Growing Up

Life used to be effortless,
when you were young.
When dreams were so immense
and everything was a song.

It seemed as if life
went on forever and ever,
kisses could heal anything,
only confined by the weather.

Why does growing up
have to be so harsh?
And since when did the world
become bigger than the backyard?

There's no more fun
and no more games.
Apparently from now
it's a life full of sorrow and pain.

Why can't we go back
to when life was our own?
Because childhood's gone
and there's no return.

Alex Williams (14)
The Mary Webb School

It's Not Fair!

It's not fair that I'm all alone,
My brother and sister have all left home
And I'm stuck in this warzone.

It's not fair that my mum barely notices me,
And my dad I don't even get to see.
Why is this all happening to me?

It's not fair that I cry myself to sleep at night,
I just wish someone would come and hold me tight,
And tell me everything is going to be alright.

It's not fair that I never get to enjoy,
Being able to be a normal, eight-year-old boy,
Who is mischievous and likes to annoy.

It's not fair that nobody seems to care,
That all I need is someone to be there,
Where are all my friends, where oh where?

It's not fair that at Christmas, the happiest day of the year,
Santa never visits with his reindeer,
All I get is a letter from Dad, I wish he was here.

It's not fair that to some people I don't exist,
I can't remember the last time I was missed,
Life has such a horrible twist.

It's not fair that people think I'm too young to know,
Exactly why my mum is feeling so low,
I've realised she needs looking after, she can't just get up and go.

It's not fair that I wish I could run away,
I don't have the guts though, so instead I just stay,
I will get out of this and be happy though, one day.

Sarah Pinches (14)
The Mary Webb School

The Tear

A single teardrop running down her face
Mournfully tracing a path,
Carved by many others before it.
Slowly following the gentle curve of her cheek,
Telling in that journey,
A tale that words cannot begin to describe,
Of sadness, woe and despair.
An account of all the things she fears.

An echo in her mind, a memory.
Curled up in a corner,
Waiting to be struck by the force of his hand,
Driven by hatred, anger and disgust.
To him she represents the things that went wrong in his life,
So he beats her over and over again.
To her, he is a monster hiding under her bed,
Haunting her childhood.

A cry in the night.
'Daddy stop, please stop.
You're hurting me, you're hurting Mummy.
We know you love us really.'
But he doesn't, his life has been a lie,
Full of drink, drugs and violence.
He runs out of the flat, slamming the door.
A gunshot. Never seen again.

Brittany Fisher (14)
The Mary Webb School

Specs

Near the beginning of my life glasses were fixed to my head,
The only time I could remove them was when I went to bed,

I was the one who always looked different,
The opticians was the kind of place that I went,

This sight-enhancing pair always got smashed,
Playing sport was the time when they got most bashed,

After seven pairs of spectacles I switched to contacts,
The small little disks of plastic could suffer no cracks,

I no longer felt the glasses perched on my nose,
Like a set of large, black, irritating crows,

The glasses had jumped off my nose and fixed themselves to Dad,
Whose eyesight for reading was getting quite bad,

My mum also took up the craze,
Wearing glasses for reading at the end of long days,

I have been in my parents' shoes,
I know what specs are like to wear and how easy they are to lose,

Two pairs of specs for my mum and dad, none for me,
But I wear them in the evenings so I guess that counts as three.

Tim Robinson (15)
The Mary Webb School

Untitled

I tend to live in the cold and snow,
In some conditions you'll never know.
My eyes are bold and my fur is fair,
I'm mostly known as a polar bear.

I roam the deserts for disused land,
Where I can rest in a pile of sand.
My skin will change to places I'm at,
The sun lights my chameleon back.

I like to swim in the waters deep,
Where in the thick coral I will keep
My children safe from sharks, whales and rays,
Searching for fish like me on the bays.

The land's 100 metres below,
I surf the wind, I sway to and fro.
I spy a worm out my beady eye,
As a bird, I sweep down from the sky.

My neck's as long as the grass is green,
My coat gives off a brown spotted sheen.
I enjoy the sun from a high space,
I'm a giraffe with horns on my face.

My slim body slides amongst soft leaves,
I snatch small mice from behind green trees.
I'm as long as a football pitch's length,
I squeeze my prey with cobra strength.

I fly from pink flower, to red, to blue,
I collect pollen on my furry shoe!
My antennae stand proud on my head,
I am a bee, on honey I'm fed.

My green arms stretch high up to the light,
I am a leaf, I stand tall with might.

Abigail Best (14)
The Mary Webb School

The Sea

As I make my journey towards land
My cold fingers pry at the sun-blasted sugary shore
I bring travellers along with me
Shells and pebbles all sharing
My everlasting journey towards the beach

The weather turns angry
And blows its fierce breath upon me
The waves I make, hit the shore violently
Like a stampede of a million horses
Retreating from some looming danger

My harsh teeth have taken many a life
I have seen many people fall from my high cliff-like shoulders
With my tearful blue eyes
The swirling movement of my current
Makes fishermen turn away in fear

The foam tips of my swaying arms
Reach, and grab at the rocks on the shore
Trying to get a grip
But my hands keep slipping away
And splashing against the seabed

Creatures swim inside my slimy hair
Combing and ripping it for the possibility of food
Seals play about
Wriggling in every direction
Having fun while they are still young

My salty tears smudge the sandcastles
Built by the children that visited my golden shores that day
My cold clammy hands drag the castles and the pebbles
In a hope that they will join me on
My everlasting journey towards the beach.

Alice Campion (14)
The Mary Webb School

The Loser

The smile is broken,
A splintered pain.
Inside the tears dwell,
Dwell in the brain.

They will not spill,
She will not weep,
They are locked away,
From her eyes, won't seep.

It is bottled up,
This pain she feels.
The door to her heart
She carefully seals.

She hides her soul
Inside herself.
She has no need
For success or wealth.

Her eyes conceal
The secret within,
For the problem is
That she hates to win.

The pressure builds,
So she can't do wrong.
She must compete,
She must be strong.

When the prizes come,
The tears don't flow.
But she feels nothing
Inside, she's hollow.

Polly Osborne (14)
The Mary Webb School

Daddy's Girl

'Oh you're such a daddy's girl!' my nan once said to me,
We'd always be fixing a bike or car, or cutting down a tree.
We'd go off to the market, I'd be given 50p,
That's how we'd spend our weekends,
My lovely dad and me.

He was the fastest racing car, the biggest, bravest lion,
He was as gentle as a butterfly but as bold and strong as iron.
And as life went on as usual, I was happy as can be,
My mum said we were so alike,
My lovely dad and me.

I'll never forget that awful date, September twenty-three,
For it was on that chilling day, my dad was snatched from me.
He'd had a fatal accident, rushed into A and E,
And then it was no longer
My lovely dad and me.

A solemn, simple funeral on a horrid, sodden day,
'Bloody awful things,' my dad would always say.
He was scattered in his favourite place, a spot right by the sea,
And we said goodbye for one last time,
My grieving mum and me.

I collected every photo and wished that there was more,
But then my mum said something that made the pain less sore,
'There's not a day we don't think of the silly things he'd do,
Or the special bond between your lovely dad and you.'

And that was when I realised, he was everywhere, you see,
There was a bit of him in all of us, especially in me.
And now for evermore, happy memories there shall be,
Of the glorious time we spent together,
My lovely dad and me.

Mollie Newbury (14)
The Mary Webb School

When I Was A Soldier

When I was a soldier,
Young and bold in strength,
I and fellow Englishmen
Fought a war of endless length.

We travelled for an age it seemed,
Over lands and seas,
To find the place where bangs and shots
Would haunt our memories.

Most of us were young and frail,
Only sweet sixteen,
Yet, not even the strongest man on Earth
Could bear the sights we've seen.

Mangled bodies, wailing cries,
The sobs, the children's screams,
These were then the noises
That shattered peaceful dreams.

We caught the drifting orisons
That fluttered past in reams,
Yet still these gentle gestures
Could not drown the booms and screams.

The tanks were large and monstrous,
Trundling with rattling sound,
The planes, fast and daunting,
Powering bombs upon the ground.

Yet being a soldier in battle
Was by far the hardest thing,
To stand and kill another man
Made you feel like no one's king.

The swish of swords, the crash of guns,
The blood upon the floor,
I remember one night thinking,
I cannot take much more.

When I was a soldier,
Young and bold in strength,
I never dreamed that I would see
Such anger and such hate.

So take time to remember
What we soldiers say,
For your own tomorrow
We gave our own today.

Sadie-Beth Holder (14)
The Mary Webb School

If Only

Cold again
another winter morning
alone and lost.
Not a penny in my pocket
not a person in my heart
if I'm dead would they notice?
If I'm alive would they cope?
My eyes are slowly closing
what more could be done?
The darkness descends upon me
there's no life left to live,
my misery has come to an end
no longer will I have to suffer.
So long, farewell
have a nice life,
I didn't.

Lucy Donnelly (13)
The Priory School

An Ode To Frogs

Frogs here, frogs there,
Frogs are everywhere!
Frogs jump, frogs leap,
Frogs peep and sleep.

Frogs are slimy little creatures
And have some very funny features
Their feet are long and webbed
And shiny black eyes that
Protrude from their head.

Frogs spring and go *ping!*
This is what they like doing.
Frogs sit upon logs
Which then get rolled by some dogs.
Oh no! then they go *splat!*
And that's the end of that!

Rebecca Bailiff (11)
The Priory School

I Wish

I look at you with sorrowful eyes,
You don't look at me at all.
Why do you walk on?
You have the power to save me.

Those who do look at me -
Look away quickly.
Almost as if it was a sin -
To glance over.

It is starting to rain.
I am sitting here with no protection.
You all raise your umbrellas and yet,
No one thinks about me.
Just because I am this way,
It doesn't mean I don't feel the same as you.

Others may assume I had hurt you in some way,
That this was all a form of revenge.
But I have done nothing
And you are doing the same.

I can't help being this way,
I beg of you to help
If I could turn back time,
I wouldn't be here today.

Stevie Sale (13)
The Priory School

Remember, Remember

They may have their steak and kidney pie
And play toy soldiers in safe and cosy bases.
Sitting there in their proud uniforms,
With their podgy red glowing faces
And their podgy bodies that have no bruises or cuts.

These are the people, who are the murderers,
Killing our brothers, sons, fathers, husbands, lovers.
Innocent lives in their hands just waiting their turn,
Turn to face the slaughtering machines
And make that long journey west with thousands of other men.

These are the men who we should worship,
The men who have lived through the real war,
Who have been to Hell and back.
They have had to live through the actions their generals have made
And seen their friends slaughtered by the enemy.

They may have their steak and kidney pie
And play toy soldiers in safe and cosy bases.
Sitting there in their proud uniforms,
With their podgy red glowing faces
And their podgy bodies that have no bruises or cuts.

These are the brutes of the First World War,
Killing our brothers, sons, fathers, husbands, lovers.
Remember, remember, 11th of November.
Remember those brave soldiers, who died for our country,
Remember, remember, 11th of November.

Anna Kramer (15)
The Priory School

Walk On By

I wake to the jangling of loose change,
Landing in the worn hat beside me,
I open my eyes
And for a moment am dazzled,
I focus on a pitiful face,
He stares for a moment, gives a sheepish smile, then scurries off,
Looking to see if anyone has seen him.
Just another day,
Just another pitiful face,
You just have to get used to it though.
They think they know everything about you,
How you came to be living like this.
But they don't know the half of it.
Some don't even bother looking at you,
They fix their gaze straight ahead
And stride right past you.
Ignoring your existence.
To them you are not there,
You are just another pile of rubbish lining the streets.

Sarah Burrows (14)
The Priory School

Waiting

Cold, the snowflakes fall on your cheek
As you call out for someone,
Someone to help you to face your fears,
Someone to wipe all your tears,
It's dark and you're frozen yet the air is sweet,
As you sit at a corner of a city street.

Some of them look down upon you,
Whereas others walk past trying not to stare,
Acting as if you're not really there.
You're their guilt, their sin,
Asking them to help fill a small tin,

Wondering whether they have a coin to spare,
Seems too much for them to care.
They could be you, it doesn't take a lot,
So they should be thankful for what they've got.

Someday you'll sort things out,
You'll get a home and travel about.
You'll have a family and cash to burn,
Maybe tomorrow it will be your turn.

Alice Welsh (13)
The Priory School

Moving On

How can it be easy to forget you?
I've tried so many times before,
To move past what happened.
I'm holding on to what I have left,
Holding on for my life.
Hoping that my grip will hold.
This is my life.
On the line.
Underneath the polluted skies,
Of lies and mistakes from my past,
That I try to forget.
This is my life support.
Sometimes there's no one there to tell you the truth,
So let me apologise when I can.
Wandering all those lonely roads,
All on my own with nowhere to go.
Be my route to escape.
Be my candle in the dark.
Be everything I want you to be.
Be with me.

Chloe Mapp (13)
The Priory School

The Bully

I am the bully,
People say I'm strong,
I'm not.
People say I'm cruel,
I'm not.
They name me on what the outside shows,
But deep down,
I have been bullied.
I am alone,
No one there for me,
Nobody to love me,
They don't see the real me,
I'm not a bully,
Just a scared person
Who needs someone to talk to,
To hold me when I cry.
Why can't they see through that 'bully'
And into the person inside?

Ellie Porter (13)
The Priory School

Alice Elle Pearl

As I look I cry,
I sob and I lie,
I say I'm fine and I say I'm good,
But as I speak I hide in my hood.
I feel as if my sun is dark,
She knows she's left her precious mark,
In all our hearts and souls,
She filled all my empty holes.
The empty, hollow space,
I picture her beautiful face,
Her curly brown hair,
It's just not fair.
She didn't have to go that way,
I picture that last beautiful day,
No one knew it would be her last,
But that's all in the past.
It still haunts me though,
I should have told her I know,
But I just didn't have the guts,
I must be totally nuts.
I didn't like the look of him,
That's all she talked about, Tim, Tim, Tim,
He was her devil, she was his girl,
I remember her name, Alice Elle Pearl.
I remember her as a sister, a friend
And worries I had she'd mend.
She still watches over me,
She has my key.
The key to my fears and wishes,
But most importantly, my heart.

Jade King **(13)**
The Priory School

Covering Up The Truth

Those scars inside,
Those scars I must hide,
Only material can hide my interior,
Stopping me from becoming inferior,
My shirt covers those holes, covering what's missing,
I can't be myself, all I've done is dismissing,
Dismissing myself, until I'm myself no more,
How do I know what is me, how can I be sure?
My true personality ebbs away,
Letting me stand and sway and think
I'll be myself today.

Edward Barker (13)
The Priory School

Alzheimer's

(For my grandma)

I wake up not knowing where I am, strange views, beyond my window,
Views I don't remember being there.
I gaze into the mirror on what appears to be a wall, my wall, my room?
Who is the old, wrinkled face looking back at me? I don't know
this person!
I touch my face, she touches hers. I can feel the lines, the short, thin,
curly hair.
I try to rub my eyes, but I can't reach them.
Glasses. When did they get there?

Who is the face I see staring back at me? I take a look around,
Pictures, triggering small remainders of memory, children, a wife,
a mother.
Now a more familiar face, the same old lady in the mirror, with these
strangers, smiling.
Seeming happy, but I know this woman, I can feel her inside me,
How I know this, I don't know, or do I? I can't remember.
But the woman, this woman, is lonely.
Confused, somehow I can relate, but how? I am but a child.
I look back into the mirror.

Who is the face staring back at me? The door opens and a flood of
children run in.
'Grandma, Grandma!' they cry. They direct their speech to me,
But they must be wrong, mistaken.
They exit to the field outside, I can see lots of old people,
Old people I can't remember,
Yet I know I have met them before. But when?
Another person enters my room, a younger woman.
I definitely know her, I feel she is part of me, an older version of me.
A voice in the back of my head is screaming, 'She is your own,
She is your daughter!'
Nonsense of course, it wouldn't make sense.
Perhaps she is my mother? I don't recall speaking to her,
But I can sense we are close. I stare into her kind eyes.

Who is the face I see staring back at me? Desperation in my
'mother's' eyes.

Desperation for what? Response?
She speaks to me as if I am young, the person I feel I am,
But I can sense more to her speech.
She wants me to acknowledge who she is. I try to speak back,
'Mother?'

But the words don't come out. I want to speak, why can't I?
I start talking faster and faster,
I am consumed with fear. Why can't I communicate with her?
There is so much I want to say.
I become tired of talking with this slur of words, so I give up.
I see the hurt behind her eyes too.

Who is the face I see staring back at me? The children run back in,
Playing with a ball.
Ah, yes, tennis I remember. 'Grandma, Grandma.'
The youngest child looks at me. Smiling, expectant, handing me
the ball.

Yes I am Grandma? And Mum? But wasn't it only yesterday
I was playing in the street?
Dirt on my hands and my cheeks? I swear it was only yesterday!

Bethany Thomas (13)
The Priory School

Lonely

I stand in the street,
begging for scraps.
There's nothing else I can do,
except watch people pass.

I am hated, I am despised,
by all the passers-by;
they look at me with disgust,
then walk on past.

I sleep in the cold,
in the cold, bitter street.
I have nowhere else to go,
no where I can be.

There is just no room,
for people like me.
No place in the world
where we can live in harmony.

Matthew Edwards (13)
The Priory School

The Carp

The carp rummages around the bottom of the pool,
Looking for food but the carp is not a fool.
The anglers bait with a hook sticking out,
But this doesn't fool the carp without a doubt.

Still searching for food in a distance away,
The carp looks and sees its prey.
The carp dashes away quick enough,
To find a strawberry red ball, tasty and tough.

The huge tail thrashes around and around,
In a splash he is on the surface he found.
Its big browny yellow scales shine in the sunlight,
Something moves above the surface to give him a fright.

It plunges back down into the brown dark,
Just ahead there is a huge shark.
This is no shark, it is another fish,
It is a pike, he knows he is the dish.

The pike opens up its mouth with a piercing look,
The carp thrashes its tail about and off it took.
The carp turns around to stop and fight,
But the pike gets scared and bolts away with all its might.

Adam Rogers (13)
The Priory School

The Furry Armadillo

The furry armadillo is a very funny fellow
Skin of blue, wings of green and fins of a creamy yellow
They live in the Asian mountains isolated and alone
Living not off leaves or insects, but off old mossy bone

Their habit, small crevices and rocky caves
Filled with fur and dust, and stinking decay
They live in packs of three or four
Maybe even five, but never one more

They are rarely spotted and quite mysterious
But if you see one don't say
As you'll be accused of being delirious

I myself, have seen many an armadillo
As I know the secrets
Like never carry the branch of a willow

Since if they smell this wooden tree crust
Not only will they sneeze
But will spontaneously combust

This is deadly as if one sees another explode
That armadillo body will also rapidly overload
And this could cause a deadly chain reaction
As the whole population, could turn into a small fraction

So if you come across this wonderful little creature
Listen carefully to this wise old preacher
Keep your distance and carry no willow
Otherwise there will be no more furry armadillo.

Matteo D'Alesio (13)
The Priory School

The Bully

I feel so sad!
I'm all alone,
No one to turn to,
Nowhere to go.

I want to die,
Your poison is running through my veins.
Why do this to me?
I'm not bad!

Start again!
That's what I want to do,
Please, I hate this,
I hate my life.

Lucy Morgan (14)
The Priory School

Bad

Mum and Dad hate me when I'm bad,
I slam the door and stamp on the floor,
Why do I do it? It makes me feel sad.

I scream and shout and run about,
I jump up and down in my nightgown,
I get send to bed, is it all for nowt?

Then I'm sad, I start to feel bad,
I sit on the chair, as I hug my bear,
'I'm sorry Mum and Dad.'

Mum and Dad hate me when I'm bad,
I slam the door and stamp on the floor,
Why do I do it? It makes me feel sad.

Sarah Youle (11)
The Priory School

My Mate

Drama queen,
Always seen,
Chocolate mad,
Sometimes bad,
Totally crazy,
Very lazy,
Superstar,
Never far,
Round the bend,
That's my friend!

Has ace dress,
Out to impress,
Helps out,
Doesn't shout,
Always wriggles,
Mainly giggles,
Respects all,
Really cool,
Has fun,
Because she's my best chum!

Caitlin Claytor (11)
The Priory School

First Day

'It's not fair,
I don't want to go,
I can't believe
You'd stoop this low.

You say that I 'need to learn',
You're acting like this is a good turn.
It's not fair,
It's just not cool,
I really didn't think you'd send me to *school!*'

'Now then child,' the teacher boomed,
Over the small boy he loomed,
'English, science, history and maths, do them well
And we'll have bundles of laughs.
Science, English, maths and DT, do them badly and anger me.'

Upon the Head's doorbell,
The small boy rang,
As she opened the door, the headmistress sang;
'Yes, what is it young boy?
My, aren't you tiny?
Like a little wooden toy,
Only much more whiny.'

'It's not fair,
I don't want to go,
I can't believe
You'd stoop this low.

You say that I 'need my rest',
I don't want it. School's the best!
It's just not fair,
Look at my face,
I don't want to go,
This school is *ace!*'

Amy Taylor (11)
The Priory School

Worm!

Worm, worm
Oh how you squirm.
Worm, worm
How you slither and turn.

Worm, worm
Where do you live?
Worm, worm
Underground so dark, but so very big.

Worm, worm
You surface when it rains.
Worm, worm
Do the birds cause you pain.

Worm, worm
So pretty in pink.
Worm, worm
Covered in soil, do you blink?

Worm, worm
So slimy and creepy.
Worm, worm
You always look sleepy.

Worm, worm
You're so boring.
Worm, worm
Writing this poem I nearly start snoring.

Annabel Minton (11)
The Priory School

Monkey

M ischievous, cheeky and a very good thief
O n the go all day long swinging from tree to tree
N ot a quiet moment with their screeching cries
K ing of the jungle they like to think they are
E ating bananas all day long
Y um, yum, yum what good fun.

Josh Stell (12)
The Priory School

Storm

The heavens break open.
The clouds get darker and darker.
The thunder gets louder and louder.
The lightning gets brighter and brighter.
The puddles get deeper and deeper.
The storm gets bigger and bigger.
The river gets flooded and flooded.
The houses get darker and darker.
The clouds get brighter and brighter.
Finally the heavens stop their anger.

Sam Robinson (11)
The Priory School

Football Match

The football match is about to start
The rain is coming down strong
Anything could happen now
Anything could go wrong.

The ref blew the whistle to start the game
I knew it was going to be tough
Because the team we were about to play
Happened to be very rough.

The ball had been moving for quite some time
Then it was passed to Joel
He crossed the ball in the box
And I scored a goal.

The teams were getting tired
Their defence line became slack
The weather on the other hand
The skies were turning black.

The ref blew for full-time
We all got really battered
I went home to have a shower
When I went to bed I was shattered.

Oliver Jennings (11)
The Priory School

Trees

Tall, short, fat, thin
so many in the world.
Leaves can be peculiar shaped,
they drop off as the seasons go past.
Brown, golden, red, green,
lots of colours to think of.
Watching it blow in the winter
and stand still in the summer.
Little animals scurry amongst it.
What is it? I wonder.

Lucie Andrews (11)
The Priory School

Under The Sea

Sea waves bashing against the rocky shores,
Snatching anything that's in its path,
With seagulls bobbing up and down,
As boats float gently by.

Seaweed swishing and swirling around,
Tangling anything that drifts along,
While underneath the lapping waves,
The fish swim slowly by.

Colourful coral, deep oranges and blues,
Slumber silently under the sea,
While creatures are hiding between the rocks,
Staying away from danger that lurks.

Hannah Davies (11)
The Priory School

Everton Football Club

Well as for the manager David Moyes,
He will sort out the boys,
Home ground Goodison Park,
The Scousers will make their mark.

Tim Cahill on the prowl,
Neville's producing another foul!
The ball's in the back of the net,
Andy Johnson's like a jet!

Now they come to the end of the game,
The Everton lads show no shame,
A few pints for the lads,
Then off home to their posh pads!

Charlie Harding (12)
The Priory School

Family

F un and friendly
A lways there for me
M um, Dad and brother too
I ll or well I still get cared for
L aughing and joking all of the time
Y ou just feel safe with them around.

Lucy Williams (11)
The Priory School

Football Crazy

My dad is football crazy,
My brother's football mad,
My mum, well she's just lazy,
But as for me I'm glad . . .
That I can play like Terry,
Although my team wears red.

Well hey a kid can dream,
What's that Mum, time for bed?

Tom Johnson (11)
The Priory School

My Guitar

My prized possession is
My acoustic guitar.
With its mahogany structure
It is my favourite thing by far.

My guitar.

When I feel angry
Or even a little bit sad
I can play my guitar
And then I don't feel so bad.

My guitar.

With every lesson I have
And every time I play
I get better and better
Each and every day.

My guitar.

My prized possession is
My acoustic guitar
With its sweet sounding melody
It is my favourite thing by far.

Georgia Yale (11)
The Priory School

The Battle Of Hastings

In 1066, the Battle of Hastings,
a gory, medieval battle to be king.
Edward died without an heir,
the next day Harold had the crown to wear.
Harold wasn't the only one who wanted the throne,
Hardraada and William wanted to make Britain their own.
Hardraada prepared 500 ships,
meanwhile William planned his tactics.
It took nine months for Hardraada to prepare his force,
house carls, footmen but none on horse.
200 miles north Harold did go,
to meet Hardraada, his Norwegian foe.
On the 25th of September Hardraada was defeated,
back to London Harold retreated.
On the 27th William set sail,
he landed at Hastings without fail.
The king gathered another army from London town,
then to Hastings to defend his crown.
A British shield wall was created,
at the top of the Senlac Hill for William, they waited.
Cavalry charged to break up the wall,
but the Englishmen still stood tall.
Into the open Harold's men were led,
for more fighting lay ahead.
With just one fire of a Norman bow,
they defeated the English foe.
With that one arrow in his eye,
the former king said his last goodbye.
From miles around you could hear,
the joyful Normans all cheer:
'Bang, bang
The king is dead,
That one arrow in his head!'

Pippa Lobban (11)
The Priory School

Football Supporters

One small ball, one big game.

Thousands of fans turn up
To see a good football game.
Winter days, summer days,
Warm days, cold days,
They turn up to see a good football game.

Supporters who are at home,
Watching the match on the television,
Cheer on their team, as if they are there.
They know that no one can hear them,
They know that they cannot make a difference,
But they still shout as if they are there.

The stadiums have rows upon rows of seats,
To cram every last supporter in,
There is enough space for them to jump up,
Shout and scream if they have scored a goal.
There is still enough space to cry
And weep if they have lost their match.

Supporters from all ages
Turn up to watch the match.
The junior supporters shouting
And screaming their heads off,
The adult supporters singing and
Eating a burger whilst doing so.

When they are walking home,
They are cheering their heads off if they have won,
Or they keep their heads down and are not talking
When they have lost.

One big ball, one massive game.

Douglas Farr (12)
The Priory School

My Grandma

My grandma was so happy,
Her life had a slow and tearful end.
My grandad lives alone
In a large and eerie house.

Sadly she was cremated,
But it was quite belated.
That made me all quite upset,
That time I'll never forget.

Before her death we all gathered around,
To see her in her final stage.
To wish her all farewell,
Soon she was to be in the ground.

Soon after her death her funeral was held
In a large and special place.
That was Meole Brace Church,
A quiet and peaceful place.

Then there was the great outdoors,
That was her final place.
That's a busy noisy place,
I know her final resting place.

Now we all shall know
Why losing someone so special,
Is a tearful time,
Let's hope that's a . . .

Jonathan Roberts (11)
The Priory School

A Dream

When you fall asleep, you tend to dream
Of a place where nothing's harder than it seems,
Of a place where no one
Has to explain what they mean.

When you fall asleep, it's often heard,
Of a time where war is an unknown word.
A place to drift to,
When your real world starts to fall.

When you start to wake, it's very hard
To remember where you travelled so far
But very soon you know
You will visit that place you often go . . .

Emily Parton (11)
The Priory School

Football

F ans cheering loud and clear
O nly the goalkeeper's in fear
O ut into the open
T alent being spoken
B alls flying everywhere
A ll but one going over there
L ots of hopes from here to there
L ots of byes, it's time to go!

Jessie Crawford Wilson (12)
The Priory School

As Fast As A Cheetah

Cheetah, cheetah flying by
Like a train on the tracks
Out to get itself a meal
After that, it's time to relax.

Cheetah, cheetah flying by
A beautiful animal about to feed
It edges closer, closer still
Then pounces at amazing speed.

Cheetah, cheetah flying by
A satisfied animal returning to rest
Lying in the shade he thought,
That deer was simply the best!

Matt Turner (11)
The Priory School

Giraffes

Giraffes are lucky they're so tall,
They make us humans feel so small.
They hold their heads up in the sky
And simply look down on us when we pass by.

Tall like a Chinese chopstick
And a tail like a balancing Libra,
Yellow in the African heat,
Its figure will take a lot to beat.

So there's the animal that sees all
Because of their height, they're so tall!

Jon Bradney (12)
The Priory School

My Dog Patch

I have a white dog
Whose name is Patch.
She's sometimes white
And she's sometimes not.
But whether she's dirty
Or whether she's not
There's still a patch on her leg
That makes her all mine.

I have a pink-nosed dog
Which is sometimes pink
And sometimes not,
Whether it is or not
She can still sniff me out
Which makes her all mine.

I have a dog who snuggles up at night,
She sometimes does
And sometimes does not,
But whether she does or not
I can tell she's my dog, Patch,
All mine! All mine!

Krystina Lyttle (11)
The Priory School

The Lion

Brightness of the eyes through the darkness of the night,
Through the long green grass of the forest - no light.
The lion spies on its prey ready to tear and bite away,
No one can escape the fear of a lion right away.

The lion is dark with its mane blocked around its face,
You would know if you saw one,
Through the clouded sky as the eyes are dazzling like a lie,
With its blacked-out face but orange and yellow eyes sunk in,
No one can escape the fear of a lion right away.

Bouncing, jumping, racing at speed,
No one can escape the fear of a lion.
The lion goes to its home when dark turns to day,
But still no one will escape the fear of a lion right away.

Laura Bowler (11)
The Priory School

Animals Of The Jungle

A tiger in the jungle lay
Silently hiding in the leaves,
Ready to pounce on its prey,
The scent of death in the breeze.

A snake in the jungle lay
Concealed in the trees,
Watching all the animals all day,
Then going out at night with ease.

A gazelle in the jungle lay
Relaxing in the shade of a tree,
Looking at the clouds pass day by day
While being stalked silently.

A cheetah in the jungle lay
Eating a leg of meat,
Watching her young jump and play,
Not bothered by the scorching heat.

Jake Westcar (11)
The Priory School

I Wish Lily And I . . .

I wish Lily and I could fly,
Reach the sky,
Sometimes I think she winks at me.

I wish Lily and I could canter across the beach,
I know she's only on loan,
But I try not to groan.

I wish Lily and I could fly,
Reach the sky,
Sometimes I think she winks at me.

I wish Lily and I don't cry,
I hope she never is to die,
And she is never to lie in pain and agony.

Martha Thompson (11)
The Priory School

Cats

Cats, cats wonderful cats,
They sneak around at night
With eyes shining like a yellow moon,
They sneak around at night.

Cats, cats wonderful cats,
They have fur so soft
With a tail propped up like a crane,
They have fur so soft.

Cats, cats wonderful cats,
They adore you with all their might,
With a miaow like a mouse being strangled,
They adore you with all their might.

Cats, cats wonderful cats,
They stuff their faces at meal times
With a mouth like a slit,
They stuff their faces at meal times.

Kirsty Winrow (11)
The Priory School

An Animal Riddle

I could be as white as a sheet
And my name could be Sam
And even if you trained me I would still not be neat,
So what do you think I am?

I can live outside in a small house
And I will round up some lambs,
My friend is someone who chases a mouse,
So what do you think I am?

You can go for a walk and I'll stay by your side,
I am a best friend to Man,
We have loads of different kinds,
So what do you think I am?

Jake Normandin (11)
The Priory School

Cheetah

Through the day this creature runs,
On the plains having fun.
To camouflage his spotted skin,
When it comes to lunch he'll always win.
No creature can outrun this beast,
You better watch out or you'll become his feast.
Any animals makes up his diet,
When he's waiting he's really quiet.
Oh what was that?
It's OK, it was just a bat.
It's not as I thought,
I'm not afraid of that,
At least it's not that ferocious cat.
You better get home to save your bum,
A more ferocious creature is your *mum!*

Megan Rowlands (11)
The Priory School

Horse

Galloping across the beach,
Kicking up sand with her elegant hooves,
With the tide going in and out as she moves.
Her tail blowing in the breeze,
See the bend in those beautiful knees.
The beach stretching out as far as the eye can see,
Nobody here just my horse and me.
With her long, flowing, silky mane,
Silver Lightning is her name.
Tossing her head as she gallops along,
With a horse like this you can't go wrong.

When we get back home I'll hose down her feet,
I've give her a rubdown and sugar lumps as a treat.

Chloe Wood (11)
The Priory School

The Snake

The deadly poisonous snake slivers silently in the sand,
Hissing and winding through the darkness,
Its red eyes gleaming in the moon.
Smooth, strong scales rubbing against the ground like nails on
                                                              sandpaper,
Seeking out its warm prey, a cold-blooded hunter.
All you can hear is the hissing of the deadly snake,
Then silence as it opens its jaw and bites into the flesh.

Lorna Yale (12)
The Priory School

The Snake

The snake slithers slowly
through the leaf-green grass.
It coils like a spring
waiting to snatch its prey.

The prey bolts hopefully,
trying to get away.

The snake sheds its skin
and grows a new skin underneath.
Then once more it slithers slowly
through the leaf-green grass,
waiting, waiting, waiting.

Rachel Burrows (11)
The Priory School

Guess Who?

She stands high and proud,
She's as tall as a tree.
She looks down at you,
But still she's friendly.

As quiet as a mouse,
She'll reach for new leaves,
Extending her neck
To the top of the trees.

Her long legs can stride
As wide as a lorry,
Running from danger,
The giraffe's in a hurry.

Tierney Jones (11)
The Priory School

I Saw A Robin

I saw a robin land on a branch,
it looked straight up at me.
All that I noticed was its big red breast
sticking out at me.
Then all of a sudden came a tweet-tweet
as if it were talking to me.
Then came a big gust of wind
and frightened him away.
That was the last I saw of him until the very next year,
but this time with the whole family.

Sonnie Bennion (11)
The Priory School

Slide Of The Penguins

Emerging from the icy sea
A penguin glances over at me
Mainly black, with a splash of white
He loves to warm up in the sunlight!

All of a sudden there were more
It was like I had opened a giant door
Down the hill they started to slide
But they'd better watch out, or they'll collide!

Joshua Dowley (11)
The Priory School

The Dahlia

A dahlia
Black and deep,
A swirling well from which tears seep,
Dewdrops lie how they glitter,
They grace the petals, a beautiful litter,
A single curl black and soft
Rests on the flower held aloft.
The last memory of a beautiful child,
Her sweet face small and mild,
Her life taken from under our sun
By the cold, heartless cruelty of the barrel of a gun.
That is why we are here,
To keep our mind's view clear,
To understand the world as a gift
And see through all its dark, dark mists.

Lottie Rapson (13)
The Priory School

A Letter For Daddy

I wish I could have known you,
Before you left my heart,
Although there's nothing I can do,
I will always love you.

It's a shame you never saw me grow up,
Or been there when I needed you.
I miss you more and more each day,
Every night I sit and pray,
Hoping you will hear me.

I wish I could have said goodbye,
Yet perhaps I was too young.
I could have been your little princess,
Why did this happen?

I love you Dad, and miss you terribly.

Lucy Church (13)
The Priory School

Storm

There was a storm last week, it was a hurricane,
It picked up cars and blew away a train.
There was a storm last week, it went off the scale,
First there was a flood, then there was hail.

There was a storm last week, it destroyed the street,
It damaged our house and gave me cold feet!
There was a storm last week, it's moved next door,
We hope it doesn't bother us anymore.

There was a storm last week, it was the size of a pup,
But a few moments later it rose back up.
There was a storm last week, it blew me away,
But I landed in my favourite place, Whitby Bay!

There was a storm last week, I was really scared,
I don't think the authorities really cared.
There's a storm next week, we've got to hide,
Or we'll all get killed, staying outside.

Hamish Spruce-Carter (11)
The Priory School

Young Writers Information

We hope you have enjoyed reading this book - and that you will continue to enjoy it in the coming years.

If you like reading and writing poetry drop us a line, or give us a call, and we'll send you a free information pack.

Alternatively if you would like to order further copies of this book or any of our other titles, then please give us a call or log onto our website at www.youngwriters.co.uk

**Young Writers Information
Remus House
Coltsfoot Drive
Peterborough
PE2 9JX**

(01733) 890066